My Tattoos

My Tattoos

Poems by

Wendy Hind

Cover art: William Hind. Acrylic on canvas designed with
syringes, scalpels, needles and thread

ISBN: 978-1-954353-89-3

Kelsay Books
502 South 1040 East, A-119
American Fork, Utah, 84003
Kelsaybooks.com

To all the parents of chronically ill children and the healthcare professionals who treat them.
To Peter, Nina, and Lexi.
To William.

Acknowledgments

Blood and Thunder Journal on the Musings of the Art of Medicine: "Make a Wish," "Flat Line"

Ether Arts: "The Snake"

HEAL: Humanism Evolving Through Arts and Literature: "The Used Heart Club"

Hektoen International Journal of Medical Humanities: "The Pump"

New Verse News: "She Who Is in Bed at Noon"

The Healing Muse: Journal of Literary and Visual Arts: "My Tattoos"

Contents

I.

HEART

The Engine

Pumping thirty-five million times a year,
two thousand gallons a day,
we rely on it to keep going.

Our eyes get to rest.
Our muscles get to rest.
Our bones get to rest.

But our heart,
never rests.

We thoughtlessly count on our heart
to keep beating –
to keep feeling.

Sometimes our heart skips a beat.
Only then do we remember,
for a second, to value its active job.

We don't remember for long.
We go about emptying the dishwasher,
going to work and getting groceries.

You'd think we would all
stop more often and
thank our hearts for beating.

For giving us
another day of life.

But like most things,
we don't appreciate it
until it stops.

Resident

When I see you come in the door,
I know you are not yet complete,
I understand you are learning,
so, please don't act like you have all the answers.

When I see you come in the door,
I know you want to appear knowledgeable,
but you must listen to me,
I know more about my child's health than you think.

When I see you come in the door,
I know you are tired,
but so am I,
and it is my child in the bed, not yours.

When I see you come in the door,
you must introduce yourself,
shake my hand,
look me in the eye.

When I see you come in the door,
treat my child like a human being,
talk to him,
ask him questions about his health and life.

When I see you come in the door,
I pray to God you have read his chart,
because if you have not –
if you have just skimmed it –

When I see you come in the door,
I will see straight through you,
and you will lose your credibility
and my trust forever.

When I see you come in the door,
be confident, yet humble.
I know you are still learning,
I know you are not yet complete.

When I see you come in the door,
I know you want to do your best
for us.
I'm sorry when I'm not at my best
for you.

The ICU Nurse

The room on the third floor feels more sterile.
The nurse, just as kind, just as caring,
but more intense than the fifth-floor nurse.
She has to be.

In the ICU there are more pumps, more meds,
more fragility of little people's lives at stake.
We will be a team for the next 12 hours.
A team that is not part of a game I wish to play.

A small body is spread eagle across the white bed.
Tiny hands with small tubes stuck into each of them.
One with juice flowing through it to keep the baby alive,
the other as a back-up, in-case the vein blows.

Sitting bedside reading, or trying to read,
I feel her presence. She is leaning against the door frame,
Her gaze alternating between the screens
and the baby. As her eyes dart back and forth,
I see her brain working.

There is no doubt she has the intellect to be a doctor.
But, she is on a different path.
She sees me looking at her.
She smiles and approaches the bed.
Her hand automatically gently strokes
the child's forearm,
brushes his hair across his head,
notices his lips are dry,
and moves his body into a new position,
so no bedsores develop.

"Can I get you anything?" she asks.
She naturally flows from the clinical
to the human.
She is a pediatric ICU nurse.

The Web

The silk strings are connected together
somehow forming a perfectly
patterned web.
Delicate, strong, magically spun.
In the center lies the prey,
stuck waiting for the predator to return.

The child's body is haloed in tubes,
flowing from various body parts.
The one out of his mouth
pushes air into his chest
while his lower lip
sags from its weight.

His eyes are closed
and swollen.
Vaseline is gently applied
to keep them moist.
He can't blink.
He has been immobilized
by the venom.

Tape and gauze secure his small body
to the web. A tiny vein in his wrist
has a silken thread protruding
where the antivenom works
to keep him alive.

Days pass. The spider returns.
One by one the tubes are taken away.
They wait to see whether the web
will need to be spun again.

The spider leaves,
not realizing that on another day,
it too will be prey.

The Pump

The pump works,
but it's leaking in a few places.
It's not very efficient.

It's been worked on several times,
but they can't seem to fix it.

Can't you try some stronger couplings?
Can't you just use a backflow preventer?
How about a compression fitting?
No?
Why not?
Keep trying.
Try harder.

It keeps leaking.

The experts tell us this isn't an ordinary pump.
They claim this pump has several strange inlets and outlets.
They say this pump has been put in backwards.

With this pump,
you can't just shut it off for a few hours to work on it.
There can be no appointments scheduled in advance,
there are only emergencies.

With this pump you can't go online and order new parts.
This pump isn't made of metal or plastic,
it's made of tissue.

This pump doesn't pump water,
it pumps blood.

With this pump,
replacing it with new parts
requires someone else's pump to stop.

The Used Heart Club

May I listen to your heart?
She places her head on my chest and is silent.
Normally, this would seem odd,
But it is comforting and I begin to cry.

I am the newest member of a very exclusive club.
With this club there are certain protocols and risks.
With this club there is joy, anxiety, and fear of rejection.

I feel very different,
and it is hard to describe.
I don't want to tell anyone what I am thinking and feeling,
But I am a new version of myself.

I swear I feel deeper.
I cry harder and I laugh louder.
If you're a member of this club you understand.

Her breath grows warm on me.
Her head is getting heavy.
She begins to weep openly and I hug her tightly.
My shirt is getting wet.

Her son's heart beats in me now.
Her worst nightmare is my greatest gift.
I am grateful and yet filled with guilt.

I promise I will talk to him.
I promise I will honor him.
I promise I will take care of him.
Please stay and listen to your son's heart.

Flat Line

A piercing siren followed by a monotonous voice.
Code blue, code blue.
Repeating, repeating.

Pounding on the door.
Get up.
Get up.

A doctor runs shoeless down the hall,
passing without looking back.
He has brown socks on his feet and
his shirt is untucked.

Everyone is running yet moving slowly.
So many people.

The masked man leaning over the baby
uses two fingers to press on his chest.
With each compression his tiny legs
lift in perfect synchronicity into the air.
The line stays flat.

I can't see his legs anymore.
He is surrounded by people.
There is so much noise.
I can't hear anything.

Then I see her coming down the hall.
She has short curly hair and big glasses.
She's wearing a sweater
and a small gold cross hangs from her throat.
She's carrying a book.

I do not speak to her.
I do not look at her.
Go somewhere else.
Help someone else.

Go away lady.
My son is not dying today.

II.

SOUL

My Tattoos

Every time I get a new mark, I stare at my body.
I try to cover it. I don't delight in my new facade. My markings are
not colorful and romantic. They are not detailed and poetic,
yet people still stare.

I received my first marking when I was very young. I have many
markings now. Some are big and some are small. Some have been
done on top of the one before. Each one is characterized by fear,
anxiety and pain.

I hate the needle, but I keep getting marked. I shake when it comes
near me. I always direct the person holding it to count to three
before they start. They promise they will. Sometimes they break
their promise.

My skin hasn't been marked with pigment, but with scars. The
artists who mark my body use scalpels. They are skilled. They are
experts. They have perfected their art. Sometimes they remember
me and sometimes they don't. I always remember them.

When I grow up, I may become the one that marks others. When
someone wants me to count to three I will. I will be gentle and
kind. I will always understand their fear, anxiety and pain. I will
always remember them.

A tattoo has been referred to as a deviant sign of something that is
absent or invisible. Absent are my spleen, gall bladder, two-thirds
of my colon and half of my heart. Invisible are my feelings,
masked by my young smile. My tattoos lie outside social norms,
but I didn't initiate them. Are my tattoos an act of deviance by
God?

I don't want any more tattoos but I'm not done being marked.

Make a Wish

Some people wish when they throw a coin in a fountain,
others wait until an eyelash falls on their cheek.

Some people wish when looking for the first evening star,
others stare into the night sky hoping for a falling one.

Some people wish when they get the big end of the wishbone,
others blow on a dandelion gone to seed.

Some people wish once a year with candles,
others whenever their necklace shows the clasp.

Then there are the wishes of children.
The sick ones.
They get one wish.

They wish to meet a pop star.
They wish to be an astronaut for the day.
They wish for a bedroom make-over.
They wish to go to Disney World.

Mostly, they wish to be out of pain.
Mostly, they wish to go outside and play.
Mostly, they wish to be normal.

Some wish for just one more day.

Night-Time Boys

As penance for leaving my son behind to go home to my bed,
I make-up the bed in the hospital for my husband.

I hate sleeping in the hospital. I hate the glow of the screens, I hate
being able to hear the nurses laughing at their station, while I look
over at tubes coming out of my son.

I hate the constant beeping of the monitors and the sound of the
blood pressure cuff inflating every thirty minutes. But most of all,
I hate how cold the hospital feels at night.

As I drive home crying, I feel bad for leaving and bad for staying
so late. We've left the girls alone again, for far too much time.

Too long for a fifteen year old to watch her little sister. Too long
for them to wonder if they were mean to their brother the last time
they saw him. Too long for them to be left to wonder if he will live
or die.

I call my husband when I make it home safely. He tells me not to
worry and to get some sleep. He reassures me our son will be okay
through the night.

They have a pact, they are the night-time boys.

The Snake

I turn on the water as hot as I can stand it. Within a few seconds the release begins to happen. My entire body is overcome with a small amount of relief and I become physically aware of my shoulders dropping.

Then the tears begin to flow. I know from yesterday that once they start, stopping them is beyond my control. They stop when they are ready to stop. They stop when they have emptied the last heartache of the day.

I cannot feel the difference between the wetness of my tears and the shower drops on my face. I'm able to wonder about this odd fact while draining away another day of hopelessness.

I press the faucet as far to the side as it will go. Willing it to go farther. Willing it hotter. Wanting the water to scald my back. A shower is the only place I can truly shed my skin. And without being able to shed my skin, and the capacity to grow a new one, I cannot carry on again tomorrow.

Lucky 7

He's small but Western-Nebraska tough.
He loves country music and football.
He wears lucky number seven on his uniform.

He hands in his exam.
He smiles,
and thanks me.

Done.
No classes tomorrow.
Time to party.

Dancing in the back of his best friend's pick-up,
he falls backwards,
out of the truck,
hitting his head on the hard pavement.

His seat is empty on Monday morning.
His seat is empty for the rest of the semester.
His strong body will never take up a seat
in any class again.

His parents pray he is not forgotten.

Seven gifts for seven strangers.
Seven people get at least one more day
to play ball with the gifts
from an angel.

Two Daughters

You were her first so she tries to inhabit your soul.
She lures you with gold seeds so you'll love her.

The second has it easier.
It's not fair.
She let her soul be free.

She doesn't use the gold seeds as a hook for her.
She gives them to the second one freely,
as a gift.

She is wiser,
or perhaps just tired.

Lying in the Shadow of Health

Lying in the shadow of health
There was a mass growing.
The pain came and went.
It was easy to dismiss.

I was busy.
Busy being a mom.
Busy working.
Busy being busy.

Lying in the shadow of health
There was a small
yet annoying
sore that would not heal.

I was busy.
Busy producing stuff.
Busy doing.
Busy being busy.

Lying in the shadow of health,
The darkness grew
until it could no longer
be ignored.

Forced to stop being busy.
Forced to face the shadow,
I can no longer avoid
my own silhouette.

The Lake Affect

When you sneak your child's muscle relaxers, for yourself,
you may have a problem.

When you start to think about a glass of wine at noon,
rather than six, you may have a problem.

When your child is in chronic pain, and the doctors have
given up, you may have a problem.

When a book comes out telling you to lean in, and you know
that if you lean in anymore, you are going to fall down,
you may have a problem.

The only thing which numbs the pain is frigid walks around
the nearby lake.

The walks begin very sad. They stay that way for a few
months.

You pick a place on your walk to stop, and look over the water
and take it all in. You give thanks for its beauty.

You notice you have begun to stop crying.

Sometimes you lose track of your thoughts now and even
notice the warmth of the sun shining on your face.

More time passes and you notice a crocus and the faint hue of
green at the tops of the trees.

You begin to think about inviting a friend on your walks. You
begin to have faith that by summer you will find peace.

The Orchid

I know its potential beauty,
because I've waited for it before.
I know it's glory,
because I've witnessed it before.

The orchid is testing me.
It rests to regain its strength.
The memory of its delicate flowers fade,
but so too does my patience.

I'm tired of performing
the Sunday afternoon ritual
of depositing three ice cubes
into its rough potting mixture.

I decide to throw it away.
Before I do,
I take the time
to look closely.

It's leaves still feel firm,
despite a thin layer of dust.
Strange new appendages grow.
Some are roots, some shoots.

The shoots produce the flowers.
I look hardest for those,
though I know the roots
are essential to its life.

I see tiny buds forming on a stalk.
It makes me pause.
The orchid
will bloom again.

Fall of Life

I've been stuck thinking
about being in the fall of my life.
With two seasons behind and
only one ahead.

Reflecting on the spring and summer,
considering if I've done enough,
have enough, been enough.
Pretty sure I have not.

Making lists of achievements,
accolades, and degrees.
Wondering if I can stop now.
Wondering if I can be calm now.

As my mind begins to quiet,
I'm able to remember the seasons
don't just come and go once,
but are a cycle of death and renewal.

Perhaps this is just one of
many beautiful endings I have lived,
providing another season
to start again.

Perhaps the coming winter doesn't mean the end,
but an opportunity to go inward,
getting ready for another spring of hope,
and another summer of growth.

Painting on the Wrong Side of the Canvas

Looking at myself in a mirror,
shows my image in reverse.
A reflection of what is actually there.

What if I've been painting
on the wrong side of the canvas
for the last fifty years?

What if the colors I've been using
don't reflect my soul's true palette?
Are they colors I let others choose for me?

The safe colors.
The primary colors.
Not the complex
and hard to name colors.

What if I've been using oil,
and acrylic,
but should have been using watercolor
or gouache?

How do you change course
this late in the game –
when bills need to be paid, college tuition is due
and expectations are so high?

Why does it take getting sick,
to remember how to be courageous.

III.

FIERCE

Rounding with the Pack

The pack comes around
early in the morning
before you can get your
wits about you.

They circle you,
pawing for a better view
in the dim light,
salivating at their newest discovery.

Deferring to the alpha,
most often a male,
some cubs mimic his bravado,
some cubs search for compassion.

The cubs are hungry.
Hungry for knowledge.
Hungry to be recognized
by the leader.

They are focused,
but tired.
It takes a lot of energy
to run with the wolves.

Before going on
to the next piece of flesh,
some of the cubs look back –
the alpha rarely does.

Talisman

For fifteen years the talisman hung from my neck
as I negotiated with God for my son's health.

If I forgot to wear it
as soon as I remembered
I'd rush to its place of safekeeping –
a tray in my bathroom –
and put it on,
judging the time off my neck as
a game of Russian Roulette.

The old Spanish coin,
with the cross faintly visible,
pressing is weight familiarly against my chest,
reassured me the bullet was still in the gun.

Only recently there came a time when
I began to question what penance
I was paying.
Would something happen to him
if I chose not to put it on?

Wearing it began to feel
like a false contract
rather than a magical protector.
More of a chain choking my neck,
than an ornament of faith.

So in defiance of my talisman,
I decided not to put it
around my neck anymore.
I waited to see if death
or hardship would fall on my son.

It did not.

His health was not related to
my wearing a coin around my neck,
or a made-up agreement with God.

Now, I choose when to wear the coin
as a reminder of our journey.
I choose when to wear my talisman
as a symbol of strength.

She Who Is in Bed at Noon

She has been too near a shooter,
She has fled a forest fire,
She has become a president,
She has lost two classmates.

She is twenty,
She is both strong and weak,
Secure and insecure,
She is happy and sad.

Home in her old bed,
She is nestled up like a cocoon,
Asleep still at noon,
Trying to repair all that's broken.

Don't let yourself fall down,
Get up,
Be present,
Be alive.

Put on your war paint,
Iron your hair,
Sharpen your claws,
Fly free again.

Fierce

It took her mother from her.
Now her chest is full of it.
She will not let it take her away from her boys.
She is fierce.

Sitting in lazy-boys, each with her own story,
She looks around the chemo room.
Whose is worse, yours or mine?
She is fierce.

After round two of that golden poison,
Her hair comes off in handfuls.
What the hell is happening?
She is fierce.

Screw you.
She will shave her entire head.
She will be in control of this.
She is fierce.

She will wear her baldness,
With big bold earrings,
And wild glasses,
And bright lipstick.

Don't mess with her
And her family, cancer.
She is fierce.

Cancer Doesn't Care

You have a maid, a food delivery service,
and a gate outside your house.
Cancer doesn't care how much money you have.

You've won a Pulitzer,
an Oscar, an Emmy, or a Tony.
Cancer doesn't care about your talent.

You can't walk down the street or
eat in a restaurant without being recognized.
Cancer doesn't care about your fame.

Your hospital is big and fancy
and your doctors all have Ivy League educations.
Cancer doesn't care about your access.

Your gown is the same as mine.
The poison entering you is the same as mine.
Your body is sick like mine.

When you are stripped,
your helplessness and pleas to God
are the same as mine.

Mammogram Souvenirs

I get my annual mammogram at a place that tries to make you feel like you are at a day spa. I know I'm fortunate my insurance covers this. After they ask me to strip down from the waste up, take off my jewelry, and wipe off any deodorant with a little wet-wipe, they give me a locker all to myself to put my bra and top and purse in. At this place, they give me a little pink wrap to put on, with a nice side tie. Very chic.

The waiting area is filled with women's magazines and these very special and expensive triangular pyramid teas with a little leaf attached to a wire to hold onto – so you don't have to fish around in the hot water and burn yourself like the paper ones.

Rarely are you alone in the waiting area. It's always quiet, with maybe some classical music softly piped-in. As new women arrive, some keep their eyes cast down, while others glance up tentatively with a weak smile acknowledging we are all here because we have to be. Acknowledging our breasts, regardless of size, are about to be crushed and contorted in inhumane ways. Acknowledging we are all here hoping we aren't the one to get bad news today.

Women are called out by friendly mammography techs one by one. Most of the time you never see the women again, but sometimes, they come back in and sit back down. This is never a good sign. It means the doctor sitting alone in the dark room doesn't like what she sees. It means you are going to have to go back in for more images.

We all know we are not at a day spa. I do appreciate that they try to make it more bearable. Less humiliating. Less haunting. Less daunting. As a consolation prize for going, some women will take a magazine – to finish the article, of course. Me? I take a few of those nice tea bags.

The Hurricane

The wind starts far out at sea,
whipping the water
like an emulsion blender,
churning the water against itself –
a force of terror
slowly approaching land.

When her will is done,
remnants of the storm
wash up on the beach –
fragments of destruction
and truth.

The tide continues to
rise and fall,
ebb and flow.
A calm is restored –
she will gather her strength
and sail again for home.

About the Author

Wendy Hind, Ph.D., J.D., writer, poet, and educator, is a former university vice president, professor, policy advisor, and attorney. She has been a guest on several podcasts and publishes health-related poems and essays in journals including *The Healing Muse, Blood and Thunder, The Examined Life* and *Hektoen International.* Her Poem "My Tattoos" was featured on New York public radio.

Hind is the founder and curator of the *tiny poetry project – narrative medicine for the soul.* She uses narrative medicine and medical humanities as a way of healing, understanding, teaching, and connecting to others regarding issues of illness and health. In addition to publishing health-related poems and essays, she is committed to teaching healthcare professionals, patients, and caregivers how to closely listen and effectively tell stories of health and illness in order to radically shift healthcare back to a whole-patient understanding – increasing the well being of all those involved in the process of healing.

Contact Info: tinypoetryproject@gmail.com
                   tinypoetryproject.com
                   #tinypoetryproject

www.ingramcontent.com/pod-product-compliance
Lightning Source LLC
Chambersburg PA
CBHW031154090426
42738CB00008B/1324